THE
CURIOUS SOFA

by
Ogdred Weary

Peter Weed Books, New York

This book has been privately printed for subscribers only in an edition limited to 212 copies, of which this is no. 83.

A perfectly plain brown paper wrapper for purposes of public concealment may easily be made at home.

Printed in the United States of America
Library of Congress Catalog Card Number: 61-12368
ISBN: 0-926637-04-5

For others

Alice was eating grapes in the park when Herbert, an extremely well-endowed young man, introduced himself to her.

He invited her to go for a ride in a taxi-cab, on the floor of which they did something Alice had never done before.

After they had done it several times in different ways, Herbert suggested that Alice tidy up at the home of his aunt, Lady Celia, who welcomed them with great cordiality.

Lady Celia led Alice to her boudoir,
where she requested the girl to perform
a rather surprising service.

Downstairs the three of them played a most amusing game of Herbert's own invention called "Thumbfumble." They then sat down to a sumptuous tea.

After he had finished the washing-up,
Albert, the butler, an unusually well-
formed man of middle age, joined them
for another frolic. Herbert and Lady
Celia had little difficulty in persuading
Alice to spend a few days with them.

In the interval before dinner she perused an album of instructive chromolithographs entitled ‚Die Sieben und Dreißig Wollüste' which Lady Celia had thoughtfully set out.

Colonel Gilbert and his wife, Louise, came in after dinner; both of them had wooden legs, with which they could do all sorts of entertaining tricks.

The evening was a huge success, in spite of someone fainting from time to time.

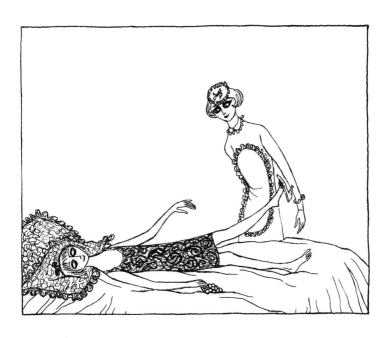

Alice, quite exhausted, was helped to bed by Lady Celia's French maid, Lise, whom she found delightfully sympathetic.

The next morning she was wakened
in a novel fashion by Lady Celia
in time for elevenses.

Looking out the window she saw
Herbert, Albert, and Harold, the
gardener, an exceptionally well-made
youth, disporting themselves on the
lawn.

They were soon joined by Donald, Herbert's singularly well-favoured sheepdog, and many were the giggles and barks that came from the shrubbery.

They called up to Alice, who, having put on an ingeniously constructed bathing slip, met them in the pool.

At luncheon, which was alfresco, Lady
Celia announced they were invited
to the Gilberts for the weekend.

To beguile the tedium of the journey,
Albert read aloud from Volume Eleven
of the "Encyclopedia of Unimaginable
Customs."

As they drove up to the house, Lucy, the Gilbert's daughter, and Gerald, her fiancé, an uncommonly well-shaped older man, emerged from an ornamental urn.

That evening in the library Scylla,
one of the guests who had certain
anatomical peculiarities, demonstrated
the "Lithuanian Typewriter," assisted by
Ronald and Robert, two remarkably
well-set-up young men from the village.

Later Reginald, another remarkably well-set-up young man from the village, provided everyone with the most astonishing little device.

Still later Gerald did a terrible thing
to Elsie with a saucepan.

The party split into twos and
threes before retiring.

At breakfast it was learned that
Elsie had expired during the night,
and gloom descended on everybody.

When a change of scene was
proposed, Lady Celia suggested
a visit to the nearby seat of Sir
Egbert, a dear friend of her youth.

When they got there, they found Sir
Egbert, an extraordinarily well-
proportioned old gentleman, and his
friend, Louie, having a romp on
the terrace.

They all went indoors and worked up
some most intriguing charades.

During the light buffet supper
Louie did a dance with a boa.

Sir Egbert offered to show them his famous sofa. Alice felt a shudder of nameless apprehension.

It stood in a windowless room lined
with polar bear fur and otherwise
empty; it was upholstered in scarlet
velvet, and had nine legs and seven
arms.

As soon as everybody had crowded
into the room, Sir Egbert fastened shut
the door, and started up the machinery
inside the sofa.

When Alice saw what was
about to happen, she began to scream
uncontrollably....